# May Day Morning in Yerevan

# May Day Morning in Yerevan

GEORGE HOBSON

RESOURCE *Publications* · Eugene, Oregon

MAY DAY MORNING IN YEREVAN

Resource Publications
An Imprint of Wipf and Stock Publishers
199 W. 8th Ave., Suite 3
Eugene, OR 97401

www.wipfandstock.com

PAPERBACK ISBN: 978-1-7252-7615-4
HARDCOVER ISBN: 978-1-7252-7614-7
EBOOK ISBN: 978-1-7252-7616-1

Manufactured in the U.S.A.                                06/23/20

To the Armenian people, bound to Christ in your soul since 301 AD. As friends and Christians, you have welcomed my wife, Victoria, and me many times to your wild, beautiful country; you have taught us much; your faith has widened and deepened our own; you have moved our hearts. We shall forever be grateful.

# Contents

# PART I

## ORANGE

Orange light of evening floods my heart.
"Lift up your hearts!" the psalmist cries.
So I do. I praise my God's great art
Unfolded on the blue infinity of sky
In cloud-waves, surf-fire, flung spume
Lobbed in bands above the western hills.
King orange reigns, Queen pink, Prince mauve looms
Where light is leaving. Profligate color-spills
Wash over heaven's ocean, roiling the sea
In blended modulations in the key of red:
Our Creator blazoning forth in glory,
Signaling that He will elevate the dead
And bathe my troubled heart with radiant light,
Banishing with beauty the encroachments of night.

## NIGHTFALL

I watch the orange sun bed down
like a potentate turning in.
The haze glows apricot a while.
Pike-like clouds idle above
the puffy hills; the trees turn
to stone, light failing. Sheep-bells
tinkle in a field, a last browsing
before sleep. Now the cooing
of doves in tree-tops ceases, the doves
fly off. Above my head a frayed
cloud-rug shows blue through holes,
lupine-colored; a gnat-sized plane
flies across a space, tying matter
to infinity with a con-trail;
but the vapor melts, the faint
thunder of the jet soon fades.
Now dark leaches sky's dome.
A few bugs flit by, black against
the pallor. A dog barks fitfully.
No wind. The birds sleep. The air
smells of hyacinth. All is still.
The silence is like a soft cloth
laid on a cradle. Night has come.

# DAYBREAK

Fresh was the day
And all the leaves shone bright
With dawn light
Swelling in the eastern sky.

Joyful was I
To see earth rise from night
And dazzle sight
With colors of a cockatoo.

Striking beams
Quicken sleep-logged earth,
Send merry mirth
Tripping down bright streams,

By green lands,
Over high peaks snow-
Ribbed, and, below,
On seas and yellow sands.

Dark ponds stir,
Sparrows dart among the leaves;
Rippling squirrels weave
Trails though gilded fir.

Creatures greet light,
Moles, badgers, cougar, deer;
They sniff the air,
They shake off cold night.

I join my voice
To the caws and croaks and moos,
To the cock-a-doodle-doos!
Oh, loudly we rejoice,

Mightily we praise
Our God, Creator, King!
Joyfully we sing:
O Lord—great are Your ways!

## RHAPSODY

I walked abroad today, full of God,
Trusting to meet Him on the May-time hills.
I saw poppies in the hedges, papery frills
Of happy orange stitched along the green-clad
Fields of nodding wheat. While my feet trod
Solid paths, yet I seemed to see the petals
Of the poppies like the fine fins and gills
Of goldfish, I striding on the bottom-mud
Of a great pond full of wondrous beings
Gliding and flitting like notes in a symphony.
Songbirds swaying on twigs exulted, piping
As the flashing fish, in joyous rhapsody,
Stole among the poppies and flowery bloomings,
All praising their Creator in sweetest harmony.

## THE WHITE PINE

The white pine wears its cones like pendulous jewelry.
When wind blows, its branches sway like Indian dancers.
Its needles, like the lashes of beautiful women,
Glitter tremulously in sunlight.

The pine is Queen. But it is King too,
As all the attendant butterflies fluttering about will attest.
With a royal eye, it keeps watch on the old stone house
And presides grandly over the garden and the lesser trees.

Appreciatively it hosts the choirs of songbirds,
Enjoying the chickadees chirping half-notes,
The soft-voiced doves, the flute-playing thrushes,
And the streaked sparrows whistling liquid calls
Or striking staccato eighth-notes.

Majestic pine, most royal and gracious,
You image the splendor of Him who made you,
To Whom, in whispered praise when the wind passes,
You bend your boughs in humble adoration.

## VAUDEVILLE IN THE WOODS

There is discussion between the oaks
And the chestnut oaks, their cousins. The oaks
Are like the proud French,
Lithe-limbed and stylish; the chestnut oaks
Are like the Swiss, their leaves heavier,
Their accent thicker. The oaks glitter
In the afternoon light, their tops crimson,
Here and there magenta, a sense of blood
Coursing through them; their cousins offer
To the sun pendulous, ribbed, gently scalloped
Leaves of green and mundane brown.
The chestnut oaks bow in the wind;
The oaks prance.

The cousins discuss the state of the woods.
How is it with the squirrel family lodged
In the hole at the base of the aging chestnut oak?
They're regular trapeze artists, both agree.
But we live longer, they add. We're venerable.
The oaks mutter that they're jealous of the scarlet dogwood.
The chestnut oaks decry the egg-yolk yellow of the maples.
Show-offy, they say. Flashy.
The oaks denounce the elongation of the hickory leaves,
Claiming elegance for themselves alone, not to be shared.
Ah, but the birds are democrats, opine the chestnut oaks
Ruefully. They fly about on all of us,
Even on those needley pines over there with their branches
That never go bare. The birds don't care.
They love us all. You're right, say the oaks,
Rustling and shimmering and dropping leaves in assent.
They're our friends, like the squirrels. They chirp nicely too.

Raccoons on the other hand, grumble the chestnut oaks,
Changing the subject on a whiff of wind—sneaky critters!
The oaks, primping in the breeze, snigger:
But their masks are chic! The chestnut oaks demur.
Then a gust sweeps the woods. The oaks shudder.
You're losing your leaves, taunt their cousins.
Look who's talking, the oaks fling back,
As flurries of brown leaves float to the ground.

Indeed. Here, there, through the woods,
Leaves are floating down. Autumn.
The seasons turn. The oaks and their cousins
Will soon stand bare in winter's cold.
Dolefully their boughs will creak,
Under snow their leaves will lie frozen.
Their exchanges will be brief and bitter:
No more merry banter,
No more effrontery.

The vaudeville will reopen next spring.

## AUTUMNAL SYMPHONY

Legumes and fruits,
Plants, grains,
Sundry spices,
Are playing chromatic music on the hills,
Fiddling, plucking, tapping, blowing.
Saffron plays violin,
Cinnamon, viola,
Mustard and cardamom, cello.
Red cabbages play double bass.
Lettuce is on the clarinet,
Kale on the oboe;
Kiwi plays flute,
Lentils, piccolo,
Asparagus, bassoon.
Avocado plucks the harp.
Squash blow the French horns,
Turnips the trumpets,
Pumpkins the tuba.
Berries tap the triangles,
Onions beat the kettledrums.
Melons clash the cymbals.

The score is the Autumnal Symphony by God.
The Composer is conducting.
Excited birds swoop and loop among the players,
Adding improvisational flourishes.
Important clouds are in attendance.
For the cows and sheep in the meadows,
There is standing room only.
Fields, ploughed and harrowed, listen, rapt;
They've had a long summer;
Half-way through the Third Movement,
They fall asleep.

# FALL SKETCHES, ON LAND AND SEASHORE

## I

Sunflowers at summer's end hang their heads like rag dolls.
Their faces go black, their golden petals wilt.
They have sung the summer through, praising God.
Like their great Creator whom they imitate,
They've shed light on the earth.
They are ready for harvest.

## II

The oval leaves of the walnut trees are yellow,
Their green veins paired like ranks of oars
On the sea-going galleys of ancient days.
They float on their branches like fleets at anchor,
Then row off in clusters at wind's behest.
They ply the bright air with their green-veined oars,
Then drop and are wrecked on the reefs of the earth,
Where they curl and go brown and collapse into dust.

## III

The ploughed and harrowed meadows
Look like pancakes on the griddle of November.
Manure flavors the air sourly.
Mushroom families in fallow fields
Imitate the Grand Mushroom in the sky.
Muddy-bellied sheep yank sparse grass,
Cows stand still like sculpted sandstone.
Heaped leaves along the country roads
Remember how it was in summer
When they shimmered gaily in sunlight

And danced the day long in tree-tops.
Now they lie like corpses on a battlefield,
Or, wind-blown, scatter wildly in terror,
Fleeing like crowds before strafing aircraft.
Their lives are over, their time is done;
They have served air, bird, insect, worm, caterpillar;
In death their leaf-life will serve soil.

IV

Boulders loom in the night at the dark ocean's edge.
Barnacles speckle the granite like stars in the heavens.
Behind the boulders, cliffs hunch their shoulders, brooding.
On the sea, starlight glitters like phosphorescence.
Wavelets lapping the sand give speech to silence.
Hidden in the enormous night, hope hides.
Earth awaits winter, holding its breath.
Spring bides its time.

## HERDS

Everywhere are herds.
Behind our house,
Yellow crocuses browse in the grass;
Above our heads,
Clouds of sheep graze in the blue meadows;
On the ploughed fields,
Glinting under late light,
Fresh-turned sods lie in clumps like Guernsey cows;
At the foot of walnut trees,
A night of frost has left leaf-herds heaped
Like collapsed stone walls;
And everywhere,
Gathered like paints on a palette,
Herds of oak and hickory and maple
Feed on the hills.

## CELEBRATING DAY

Everything is celebrating day.
The red clouds clap as the sun
Pokes up from earth like a crocus shoot
And flowers in the eastern sky.

Birds, big and little—
Crows, larks, swallows, doves—
Streak through the morning air
Like arrows in an archery display.

Their black shadows race across the earth,
Leap the fences,
Speed up and down the walls of the stone houses,
Sail magically through tousled trees.

Shadows of oak and sycamore
Bunched on the meadow's edge
Caress with tapered fingers, tenderly,
The furrowed faces of the fields.

Under a breeze, shadows of walnut trees
Shiver on the frosted ground,
While the few leaves left on the branches
Fly off like flocks of birds.

Winter—summer's shadow—is coming.
Lively green and sun's yellow heat are memories.
Brown reigns now, cold stalks the hills.
The constellations are moving house.

## LAST CELEBRATION

Fall.
It's time for a last celebration.
The trees are taking their clothes off.
Thousands of still-leafed limbs rock in the wind,
A polyphony of motion.
The oaks shower confetti on the roads.
The limes drop old pods,
The pines, cones.
Sycamores wave their thick arms.
Unpicked walnuts, once pea-green,
Now blackened and wrinkled like widowers,
Shells cracked,
Litter the roadsides and groves.
Wind herds leaves on the highways,
Like cowboys herding cattle.
It bulldozes leaf-humps, corrals foliage.
Wind is scrupulous,
A taskmaster:
It scours nature,
Putting order,
Tidying up for winter.
The celebration is nearly over.

## WINTER

Corn-stalks totter on the frost-bound hills
Like Napoleon's stricken soldiers stumbling
Out of Russia, where despotic cold kills
Bird and beast and presumptuous men, fumbling
Their way homeward on the cannon-rutted plain,
Freezing hard as boards in the ghastly snows.
So those who bravely strutted once lie slain
Now, doomed by war and winter's deadly blows.
Is ice only cruel? Do not its keen blades gleam
With heaven's light and speak of lovely hope,
All set, awaiting Winter's thaw to stream
Out in joy, when the poor, raised up, shall elope
With their great Lord? These stalks in sad array,
Ice-clad, point, for seeing eyes, to glorious Day.

## SHADOWS

Winter light, late afternoon.
Our shadows walked across the green and yellow fields
Like figures on stilts.
On stilts we leaped fences,
Strode among raucous patches of juniper,
Slipped through prickly blackberry bushes
Without drawing blood.

Our shadows were long blades opening and closing like scissors.
They were fixed to our feet,
Weightless extensions of our bodies
Reaching at right angles eastward while we walked south.
As shadows, we passed soundlessly
Where heavy machinery had labored earlier,
Ploughs, discs, harrows;
We moved like air in the ruts made by huge-wheeled tractors.

"We prove," our shadows spoke up abruptly, "that you exist.
You block light. You are matter."
They added playfully: "So you *matter*."
Almost wistfully they went on:
"You are graspable, huggable.
We aren't. We're simply signposts
Signaling the wonder of material reality.
We're prophets, no more," they went on.
"We point to bodies."

Startled at this, we stopped walking.
The air was perfectly still.
For a minute our shadows were silent.
Then leaves fluttered in a puff of wind,
Our nostrils smelled mint,
Our eyes took in the checkerboard meadows
Stretching away to the hills,
The hills rolling like waves to the horizon,
The horizon emptying out into blue sky.
We saw a crow in a juniper bush,
Our ears heard caws.

Suddenly our shadows broke the silence:
"Bodies are solid," they cried out.
"They are under light."
The shadows paused, then added softly:
"And light is love made visible."

Their words reverberated in the still air.
"We are here to declare that you are," they whispered,
Gripping our feet with an infinite tenderness.
"You *are*!" they repeated.
"And that means you *are loved*."

# PART II

## CRAFT

Time is a pen in our Creator's hands,
Space his paper. He traces bold designs
On the vast blank, limns features—lands,
Suns, seas, forests, fish—all creatures—lines
On the emptiness of white, curling and coiling
Under love's press, as the pen on the sheet
Drafts populations out of dim, roiling
Forms forged in unimaginable heat.
Us too he sketches patiently, from womb
To birth, through youth and the ripe years to death,
Modelling us for life beyond the tomb,
By sure craft shaping us till our last breath.
So with time we're drawn, and finest art,
To live outside time's range, inside God's heart.

## TIME

Here we are at a turn
on the road of time, for time
is a road turning, going on,
going forward, winding
towards the End that is the Beginning,
bending out, in, buckling,
bearing worlds gone cold,
their music still echoing
like the rush of waters
in deep mountain gorges,
and bearing worlds to be,
portents of Dawn, like the words
of the Angel Gabriel to Mary.

Now time does straight shots through prairies,
now hair-pins in the mountains.
It punctuates the discourse of space,
adding commas and colons to forms,
but never full stops anywhere,
never dead ends,
unless we speak of the dead by the trillions
heaped up where time has passed by.
Here is evidence of something wrong,
something not just past but not right,
not time itself but something inside it,
something inside time needing fixing.

Time itself can't do the fixing,
for time's a traveler, not a savior,
it moves,
goes on,
journeys,

now slow like a tortoise,
now swift like a cheetah,
sidling, galloping, crawling,
restless,
never sleeping,
it goes on,
goes.

By night time creeps through slumbering populations,
through earth's trees, rocks, seas,
over myriad beasts humped in sleep like stones;
by day it courses through agitated cities,
riding incognito on the humming machines,
bearing like a tide the concoctions of humans,
raising up, wearing down,
renewing and destroying the generations of men.

Time goes,
goes forward,
goes somewhere—
it is no circle.
Its course implies an end, a destiny,
hinting at purpose
inside the contingent.

But what's wrong must be fixed:
a Bird must plunge down out of heaven
and die down here with the trillions,
then rise up and soar.
Time too is infected,
it too must be saved;
only its Source can redeem.

And so He did, does, and will come.
Time's End is the Beginning that already is and will be,
the assembling of the sundry creations on its journey,
offered, transformed, to its immanent Maker,
become then the substance of God's manifest Kingdom:
earth and heaven married—
the New Creation.

## LOW TIDE

Man's old illusion, lodged in the mind like a cyst,
Is to think his nakedness is clothed by being known.
Our mastery of nature never made a star exist,
Nor mountain, humming bird, nor fleck of foam
Upon the fig-blue sea. We seed clouds and make rain
Fall: blithely take the credit, though no man
Made the rain. Above and under all reigns
God, not Law, nor yet the man-made Pan:
Reigns Christ, who had to come amongst us to enlist
Our faith—for how shall mere flesh own
God Lord unless this Lord himself our pains
Of flesh has borne, bringing mortality within his span?
That we should know the temperature of suns
Does not assuage our loneliness or heart's pinch
To hear the seagull shriek where the tide runs
Out-in-out relentlessly, winched
By the sea-pulling moon, and this by no
Decree of ours. For us that pulse shall cease
One day, at rise or fall of the ocean's flow:
This we know. But knowing offers no release,
No answer, only fear that strikes and stuns
The mind and makes the proud heart flinch
And then put on indifference or fancy show
To camouflage the terror, the telling crease
Upon the haughty brow. We suffer loss
Because we fear to lose, or loose, control,
As if we had control to lose; we gloss
With fables life's plain texts; our buttonhole
We stuff with plastic roses, gaudy-petalled.
And then we watch, not seeing, as the tide drops: as tins
And caps and bottle-tops emerge, settled

On the algae and the drowned sea-rocks, the sins
Of our fathers and our own. But these we're blind to: the dross
We see as pure; the fool's gold on the shoal
Of our crippled years, as true; our hearts, as metalled
With the ore of kings. But see! The tide, rising, grins.

# BLOOD

Sumac by the wall of the country church was carmine.
Blood squirted when wind shook the leaves.
One thought of Christ's head being pierced by thorns.
Blood stained the inside of the church too,
Where light through the colored windows melted on the stone floor.

The silence in the nave was heavy with age.
Centuries of faith had the odor of nutmeg.
Hundreds of phantom figures sat in the benches,
Heads bowed.

The central aisle stretched East to the choir.
At the topmost tip of the transept arch
The beaks of two swallows poked out of a nest.
Suddenly the birds burst forth like rockets
And flew joyfully up and down the nave.
Finally they circled the altar
And settled again by their nest.

The side of the Christ on the tall cross behind the altar
Was caked with blood.

## FLOCKS

A flock of crocuses is grazing on the parched lawn behind the house.
Yellow-petalled cups beseech heaven:
"Give us rain!"
On the road a flock of skinny sheep trots by,
A tide of wool.
Some limp.
"Baaaa! Baaaa!"

Elsewhere sheep are being slaughtered.
Rape
Torture
Murder

In the wilderness of the world
Flocks of human sheep are following their Shepherd
Through narrow gates into green pastures.
Night falling, wolves gather, salivating.
They leer and growl.
They have stone eyes.
The sheep *baaaa* hymns to keep the wolves at bay.

Suddenly—terror!—a fork of lightning cracks open heaven.
Thunder booms,
Clouds explode.
The wolves flee, some drop dead.
Torrential rain inundates earth.

On the lawn behind the house,
The flock of crocuses raise their yellow cups
And drink.

## FIRE OVER THE WORLD

Fire over the world,
Our darkness breeding hell;
Under our smug well-
Being, hell-fire unfurled.

Our warrior race wields
Steel; we clash, we hate;
"Peace! Peace!" yields
Few gains; we rage: our fate.

Our fate it's not. Our *choice*
Brings down hell. "You", we cry,
"Are evil!" So we kill. We die.
Ah, but we could rejoice!

Rejoice in women's beauty,
Not defile it; in man's strength,
Not destroy it; of love, make duty's
Pleasure; to great length

Go gladly for the other. But no,
We're killers for whatever cause
Possesses us, whose laws
We fashion to define the foe.

We seek out foes to nail.
Darkness deepens round us, lit
By awful flames: the wail
Of women, men's howls. The pit

Of hell yawns, devours. We die.
Over the world, under it, fire.
In Beauty, a voice: "Why
Do you hate me? My desire

Is *for* you. I died to give
You life. I shared your night,
It's mine too. So let me live
Inside you—I'll be your light."

Words echoing in our cave,
Words bouncing off our walls.
Whom will Beauty's cry save?
Who will hear His calls?

## REFUSAL

It's Advent, Lord; soon you'll come to us
Again. I rejoice with the shepherds and angels. Yet
Tonight I'm sad. To think you came to us
And we refused you, makes me weep. I met
My own sin on a dark night once, it did
Me in; but you gave grace, I saw your love,
I welcomed you. When I fall down, you bid
Me rise, and I do. But my *race* won't move.
We refuse you! We scorn you! We nail you again
To the Cross! Ungrateful creatures! This makes
Me weep, Lord. Yet each year you come. Our sin
You keep bearing, in mercy. My heart aches:
*We won't believe!* And so from age to age
We live in death and spit on you in rage.

## AVALANCHE

I

Towering configurations in the sky
Convolutions
Concatenations:
*Mirrors of the soul.*

Dramas staged by cumulus
Altocumulus
Cirrus
Cirrostratus
Cirrocumulus
And nimbus's wet blanket:
*Reflections of consciousness.*

Hooks
Filaments
Tufts
Patches
Splotches
Stepping stones paving the road to infinity
Lamb's wool swaddling the bleeding sun
Laminae, almonds, mosaics:
*Fluctuations of emotion.*

And—see the lively mind's range:
To east herds of altocumulus grazing in azure fields
To west gaunt dogs scavenging in ruined cities
To north giants building towers
To south a whipsaw sprouting teeth along the horizon
*Imagination's merry-go-round*

## II

But now there is ominous movement in the heavens.
Cloud-crowds are gathering.
Rumblings
Slippages
Cumulus are flexing their muscles.
The air tightens.
Suddenly the sun disappears,
Shadow swoops down,
Wind attacks.

## III

And out of the blue—
All at once—
Upheaval.

*Avalanche!*

Huge bundles of cumulus come loose abruptly from sky's mountain,
Catapulting down the slopes;
Whole cliffs collapse;
Great bolts of cotton roll down,
Sacks,
Huge bags of flax,
Billows, pillows,
All heave, tumble, careen down the sky.

And on the blue plains gigantic cauliflowers pile up,
Colossal vegetables;
Cloud-chunks sag like bombed buildings;
Monstrous brains are strewn in the valleys.

*Heaps*
All is heaps
*Heapsheaps*

I am hollowed out,
I am bones,
Ash,
A shadow

Oh the end! The end!

*My God!*

On the mountain not a sound can be heard

# PART III

## MAY DAY MORNING IN YEREVAN

I

In this pulsating land,
Where you feel the heart beating and the pumping blood
As if the stone itself bore blood,
Blood and fire,
Memory of its womb,
Molten,
Its birth in tumult—
Here where men are stocky and strong
Like the blocks of tuff they build their churches with,
And the tight-trousered women in black heels have obsidian grapes for eyes
And for lips sections of blood-orange—
Here I went out this May Day into fresh morning,
And saw the poplars painting leaves on Yerevan's porcelain dome,
And pussy willows full of tenderness,
And tulips flaring near the doorways of dank apartment blocks
Built in Soviet times.

I saw the girls in pairs, arm in arm, dark-lashed and lovely,
Insouciantly parading their oval eyes and ruby mouths,
And the clutches of young men dressed in black leather,
Compact, hair close-cropped, macho and gentle,
Sober beneath their male jocularity.
I saw couples strolling on the potholed avenues beneath the larch trees,
The shadows of bright leaves flowing over them like water,
Or sitting on benches and at parasoled tables in parks,
Floating in each other's eyes.
The children played like children anywhere,
Bouncing about like pogo sticks,
The girls shrieking, the boys shouting—
Yet somehow they were different,

Like no other children anywhere;
The wells of their eyes held dark depths
No sun could reach.

II

It was not here that the worst of it happened,
the Great Catastrophe,
the '*Medz Yeghern*',
not here in the Caucasus
(though here in the Caucasus,
in the Socialist Republic of Armenia,
Stalin martyred the Armenian Church in the 30's,
to complete the Christ-hating work begun by the Ottoman Turks)—
No, it was west of here,
in the cities and deserts of Anatolia,
where in the course of two years,
1915–1916,
at least one million three hundred thousand Armenians,
out of the one million eight hundred thousand Armenians
living in the Ottoman Empire,
were systematically exterminated
by order of the Young Turk government.

*Speak it out of memory, old woman*
*Speak it from the documents, old man*
*Speak it from the memoirs*
*The official reports*
*The letters—*
*Speak it*

The Armenian elite of Istanbul were arrested on April 24, 1915.
Many were hanged from gibbets in the city streets;
others—as recorded by the infamous photograph on display
in the Genocide Memorial Museum in Yerevan—
were led away by Turkish soldiers gripping long rifles.
None was ever heard from again.
That was the beginning of the planned decimation,
the definitive, irremediable extirpation,
of the Armenian people by the Young Turk government.

*"On the basis of the huge amount of information we possess," says Krikoris, "we are making our report to posterity. Our enemies cannot succeed in denying it forever. More and more voices will speak out, like streams trickling down a mountainside. The voices will build to a roar, the streams will swell to a river." The historian pauses. There is a long silence. His eyes roam across the past, then come to rest on an open window in his room that gives out on a wide field. "Someday a critical mass will be reached," he says. "Then all at once everyone will be talking about the Armenian genocide, and suddenly it will become a reference point to make sense of the history of the Twentieth Century. All the horror so long repressed or pushed aside will be shouted from the rooftops. I don't say I will see the day myself, but it will come."*

In the same period, thousands of loyal Armenian citizens of the Empire, inducted into the Ottoman army to fight against the Russians, were disarmed and taken away in small groups to be shot. Any effective resistance to the planned genocide of the Armenian people was thus disabled from the start.

*"Yes," says Krikoris, "the Young Turks were much better organized in 1915 than Abdul Hamid in 1895 and 1896. The Sultan of the disintegrating Ottoman Empire did manage to teach the Armenians a lesson (a handful had rebelled because of Abdul Hamid's refusal to implement reforms demanded by the European powers, and had forcibly occupied the Ottoman bank in Constantinople to incite the Europeans to react and put pressure on the Empire). His troops massacred a hundred thousand of them in retaliation for their effrontery, and caused several tens of thousands more to die of cold and hunger; he destroyed more than two thousand villages and forced thousands of refugees to flee northeast towards the Caucasus." Krikoris waves his hand in the air. "The whole thing was efficiently carried out, mind you—but compared to the methods of the Young Turks twenty years later, the Sultan's operations were scattershot. In the last hundred years, each government attempting genocide has learned from a previous one. Operational expertise, you might call it. It's the democratic nations—the nations that could prevent such horrors—that never learn anything. Vital interests and all that. Hitler learned a lot from the Young Turks, just as the Young Turks had learned from Abdul Hamid. 'Whoever today remembers the Armenians?' the Führer is reported to have said to his henchmen as they prepared the Shoah. Indeed." Krikoris frowns. "It's a comment that bears thinking about."*

Wholesale massacres and deportations proceeded apace,
first across eastern Turkey, then in the west.
The enterprise was carefully orchestrated,
a model for its Nazi successor
(and for Pol Pot in Cambodia
and the Hutu extremists in Rwanda).
The Armenian populations in the towns were rounded up:
the men were separated out and shot or hanged,
the women and children were deported in convoys
towards Cilicia and the Syrian desert.
In the west, if the towns were near railroad lines,
the Armenians were packed into cattle cars and sent south;
in the towns farther north, near the Caucasian front,
they were summarily massacred on the spot.
All their goods and property were plundered by the Turks.

*"Our murderers were crass thieves," said Hagop, the poet.*
*"But their motives went deeper than greed.*
*If you would deny the existence of someone,*
*you must do more than kill him;*
*you must eliminate his memory—*
*and that means destroying every trace*
*of his passage through life."*

The convoys spread out across the Anatolian plateau,
old men, women and children by the hundreds of thousands,
with no food but the little they started with
or could glean on the way.
Half of them died of starvation or thirst
or simply dropped from exhaustion.
At the whim of the guards they were tortured, whipped, raped.
Local populations of Kurds or Turks attacked them
as they passed through their towns,
sometimes keeping a number as chattel.
It took the Young Turk Ittihad in Istanbul,
directed by Talaat, Enver Pasha, and Djemal
(true believers in the myth of Panturkism),
less than a year and a half

to empty out the Ottoman provinces of Armenians
(who had been there for two millennia
before the arrival of the Ottoman Turks)—
*Erzeroum, Bitlis, Trebizond, Sivas, Diarbekir, Kharpert,*
*Angora, Brousse, Ismid, Andrinople, Yozgad, Caesarea, Adana—*
and turn the plains and mountains of Anatolia,
from the Black Sea to the Taurus Range,
into boneyards.

*As in the days of Herod,*
*Archetypal slaughterer of innocents*
*(So reports Matthew the Evangelist),*
*A voice is heard in Bitlis,*
*Weeping and great mourning,*
*Armine weeping for her children*
*And refusing to be comforted,*
*Because they are no more.*

The last stage of the Ottoman genocide
was organized in the province of Aleppo,
where what remained of the convoys converged.
The skeletons still living were parked in camps
and then sent west towards Deir-es-Zor.
Zeki Bey imposed an artificial famine,
and tens of thousands perished in the Syrian desert.
Witnesses reported that between Meskene and Deir-es-Zor
The road was paved with corpses.
Encampments of crazed survivors
Were strung along the banks of the Euphrates,
at Haman, Rakka, Sebba, Abou-Herrera, Deir-es-Zor,
where caravans continued to arrive weekly.
On orders from Abdulahad Nouri,
guards and the ever-active *tchété*
(thugs released from prison for the cause)
murdered thousands every day and threw them into the river
or loaded them, tied together, into boats and sank them.
The muddy banks of the Euphrates and its tributaries
are chinked with bones to this day.

This was the final solution to the 'Armenian Question',
precursor to that other 'final solution'.

*Over the thousands of unnamed dead the wind still softly moans:*
*Over men's free choice to hate Him who is Other*
*Over men's free choice to hate those who are other*
*Over men's fierce hatred of themselves for hating—*
*Over these roots of unnameable cruelty*
*The wind still softly moans*

## III

We should not forget that in the deep darkness
that covered the Ottoman land,
there were also righteous Turks and Kurds,
men and women who risked their lives
for their Armenian neighbors
and gave them refuge
or refused to obey orders to assassinate them.
Their reward will be great in heaven.

*"My grandmother never knew his name," says Astrigh. "But for four days*
*running, on the track out of Ourfa, the burly Turk with the black eyes and*
*eyebrows like bushes brought her and her sisters food and water. Why? Only*
*God knows. It was not well looked upon by the captain, but the man had*
*authority. Still, he took a risk. Because of him, they survived. They made it*
*to Aleppo, where a Syrian banker took them in. That's why I can tell you this*
*today." Her gaze crosses that of Hagop and Krikoris. "We must speak what we*
*know, must we not?" Silent nods.*

## IV

In the monastery of the Holy Precursor of Mouch,
the priests and bishops were shoed like horses by Djevdet's troops,
then gunned down or burned
with the rest of the monks.
Such actions were common under Djevdet's command.

Mustachioed police and uniformed guards
enjoyed making women dance naked in public squares,

(having ravished them beforehand, if possible),
then dousing them with petrol and torching them,
so that their hair exploded like dry bushes
and their heads turned into balls of fire;
their bodies slowly shrivelled and went black,
then their bowels spilled out on the ground
like stuffing from cushions.

Pregnant women were eviscerated
and their babies sliced in half.
Other women, having been raped,
had their breasts cut off
and knives thrust up their vaginas;
the guards watched, expressionless,
while the women writhed, fainted,
and slowly bled to death.

It is recorded that on some of the convoys in the Syrian desert,
the severed hands of children lined the beaten tracks for miles.

V

At the end of the world,
Near the Syrian-Iraqi border,
Gouged in the desert
Like a gash in a corpse,
Is the cave of Shadaddie.
Here, in a composite of mud,
Clay and ash, are more bones.
Turkish guards raped the desert
By stuffing this uterus of rock
With thousands of Armenians,
Thus facilitating their untimely birth into heaven.
The guards piled scrub at its entrance,
Set it on fire,
And kept watch all night.
In the morning they went to the nearest town
And got drunk.
One small boy in the depths of the cave

Had enough air to breathe
And survived.
After three days
(The length of time it took Christ to harrow hell)
He crawled over half-burnt corpses,
Through ash and flesh,
And escaped
To tell his tale.

Are there other Shadaddies
In the Syrian desert?
We don't know,
No witnesses lived to tell us.
But in the storehouse of the Turkish soul,
Where the past, like its victims,
Lies savaged and mutilated,
Maggots breed in the stacks of flesh
Flung into dark corners
And rotting under shredded tarps.

VI

*Those cowards shall not live, says the Lord,*
*And they who build their glory on a lie shall die.*
*The truth shall be shouted from the housetops,*
*It shall not be concealed forever.*
*Those who denied shall be denied,*
*Those who cast out shall be cast out,*
*Those who tore my children's flesh shall be torn.*
*Their children and their children's children shall not prosper,*
*They shall stagger and not find their way,*
*I will make them drunk until they humble themselves,*
*Until they speak truth instead of falsehood,*
*Until they have the courage to renounce the lie*
*They build their glory on.*
*Their glory is like a hollow gourd, says the Lord,*
*And I will break it into pieces.*
*But if they do admit their sin,*
*I will have mercy on them and give them grace,*
*Though they do not know me or acknowledge me.*

# VII

*Look*:
On the sea-floor of consciousness,
Far below appearances,
Far down in dark,
Oppressed by leagues of water,
*Here we are.*
We are here with our brothers the worms,
Crawling around.
Here we see nothing, hear nothing,
There are no echoes down here.
Far above, on the surface,
Steamers pass, waves roll,
People in sailboats kiss.
We do not hear them, we do not see them,
We cannot even imagine such things.
This is the bottom, where we are.
Down here we are not seen,
We are not heard.
If there is actually a world up there,
We have forgotten it,
It has forgotten us.
We crawl around with the worms, our brothers.
Only the worms know we are here—
The worms and God.
God knows we are here.
He made us in his image.
With us here, on the bottom,
Is the Word, God's Son.
The Word has become like us,
In the eyes of the world despised.
He is our brother.
Because he has made us in his image
And is here with us,
We have dignity.
In this utter **NO**,
He says to us gently,
Gently and with great power: *"Yes"*.

We know God is here.
Far above, they do not know that.
They do not even know he is *there*—
They certainly do not know he is *here*.
They do not know he became like us
To be with us.
They see nothing, hear nothing.
Down here in this world as men have made it,
In this sunken waste of death,
In this heart of human reality far below appearances
And the veneer of culture,
We hear, though deaf,
We see, though blind.
And we live, though we drown—
And *we shall live.*

*For we are loved*

VIII

O my God,
I have wept,
Wept—
But I do not weep any more.
I can't.
My strength is gone.
You know—I had no food for my boy,
My dear little skeleton, my Vahan.
I couldn't feed him.
One night he was snatched from me
And they cut off his hands.
He whimpered and bled to death as the guards held me down.
Then they urinated on my face and kicked me and laughed.

This is the end of the world.
Has the devil won?
Has he defeated my Lord?
Why do you tarry, Great Savior?
*Why don't you come?*

We are your people,
We name your Name—
So we must suffer as you did.
As men hated you, so they hate us.
The disciple is not above his master,
You told us that.
You promised to reserve a place for us in your Kingdom,
Where all will be well.
I believe your promise, Lord,
In it lies all my hope.
I trust you, come what may.
You are my star,
My heartbeat,
My life.
So, Lord, I dare to ask you:
*What are you waiting for?*
What horror must we know
Before you come in glory to fetch us?
Why do you not put an end to it?
*What holds you back?*
This is my complaint,
Which I whisper to you desperately
As I lie here alone on the cold sand
Under this enormous night
Full of cold stars,
Alone,
Alone beyond imagining,
Near-dead,
Shrunken,
Filthy,
Stinking with urine,
My child tortured and murdered.

I can't shout, or I would.
*I would shout, Lord,*
Oh, I would!
Lord, *how long?*
Rain down fire on these outlaws!

Judge them!
Why do you allow such cruelty,
Cruelty beyond conceiving?
*We don't deserve it!*
*We did nothing to merit such horror!*
But of course, you know that—
You didn't deserve it either.
No—but you suffered your trial and Cross for some purpose, Lord—for *us*!
Even for *these killers* who hate you!
But for whom are we suffering, Lord?
And for how long?
What possible meaning can our agony have?
Oh, I would shout, Lord, I would:
*How long?*
*How many centuries upon centuries?*
It's too much—we can't bear it any longer.
*Do you hear?*
*Do you hear me, Lord?*
*Why don't you answer?*

I would shout, I would.
But I'm too weak to shout,
Too tired.
Just bones.
They'll kill me soon,
I'll be dust soon.
Ah, Lord, then I'll find my child and husband:
Little Vahan,
Ashtot—
I'll be happy.
Ashtot, murdered at Kharpert—
By Sabit Bey's troops.
*I Remember.*
We'll rejoice together.
And I'll find *you*.
I'll see you face to face.
And I'll tell you straight off, O my Lord—
Oh, I will!—

I will beg you to return in power and glory
To take over your world—
And to come *quickly!*

My God, we're having a hard time of it,
A hard time.
We're almost finished.

O my dear
My dear
My *Savior*

*Quickly*

My dear

*Come*

*quickly*

I am a voice in the wilderness
Crying
A voice
Crying
A voice

Dying

*Thy Kingdom*

*Come*

*Jesus*

# IX

Under the larch trees the couples walk arm in arm.
People are playing tennis in the municipal courts.
Cats chase each other up a tree, squealing.
Children play hopscotch in a back alley
Behind the tin-roof houses
Where the washing is stretched
In colorful squares along the concrete balconies.
The Soviet era is finished,
The citizens of the Republic of Armenia
Are savoring their freedom.
They try to forget the earthquake of 88,
When thirty thousand died in Spitak and Gumri.
They try to forget the winters in the early 90s,
When so many young men were falling in the Karabakh war
And the Turks and Azeris blockaded the borders,
So that food and electricity and water and wood were scarce,
And there was no heat at all, month after month,
And the cold crept into the flesh and stayed there,
Like a squatter in a derelict house.

*Is there no end to our sorrow?*

But this morning in the sunny streets of Yerevan
The girls with blood-orange lips step lightly,
Spring is in the air,
And Mt. Ararat, *our Ararat,* in the west,
Like the heavenly Father
Embracing his Son
When he died on the Cross,
Spreads its arms of snow
And enfolds its people,
Oblivious that it stands on Turkish land
For the time being,
Just west of the border
Of the Armenian Republic:
Our precious holy mountain
Given by the Soviets to our murderers

By the Treaty of Kars in 1921,
In exchange for assurances that Batoum,
The terminal port for the pipeline from Bakou,
Would be theirs.

X

O my soul, *my soul*—
Comes now the question
At the void's black center,
The question that alone can frame meaning
In the vortex of darkness,
Enfold broken shoulders
In a mantle of grandeur,
Haul from the torment
Bright vestments of glory—
*Can you forgive?*
*Can you learn to forgive?*
*Can you want to learn to forgive?*

**"How many times shall I forgive my brother when he sins against me?"**
**asked Peter. "Up to seven times?" Jesus answered, "I tell you, not seven**
**times, but seventy times seven."**

Lord, the Turks are not my brothers.

**"You have heard that it was said, 'Love your neighbour and hate your en-**
**emy.' But I tell you: love your enemies and pray for those who persecute**
**you, that you may be sons of your Father in heaven."**

Lord, I can't.

Yes, you can. I did. Through me, you can.
You must *will* to. Forgiveness is not a feeling,
it's an act.

I can't.

No, it's that you don't want to.
Your wounds are too great;
you fear justice will never be done if you forgive.

Until they admit what they did—
what their ancestors did—
what they continue to do by denying what their ancestors did—
I will not forgive.

You must give them grace, as I did to you.
You must forgive first,
in your heart,
in your hearts as a people,
even before they admit what they've done,
even before they admit their evil.
Then, with time, they will acknowledge it.

How can I know that?

You can't; but it is the way of the human heart.
As long as you accuse them,
they will defend themselves and resist you.
Condemnation only breeds self-justification.
If you give them grace,
you release them to see what they've done.
Channel your anger towards grace, not revenge.
Justice never comes by revenge.

And if they continue to deny the truth?

They will remain slaves to their sin,
unable to find peace as a nation.
Unrecognized guilt will shackle them;
their souls will remain divided.
That is the way for people who live a lie.
Those who deny the truth are slaves,
victims of their own deceit.
But as for you,
you will have freed yourself;
those of your people now bound by hatred
will be released.

And if I don't forgive?

The Turks will have defeated you twice:
first, by their abominable crime;
second, by holding you captive to bitterness.

But how can grace ever bring about justice?

If the assassins were still living,
they would be brought to trial,
as in Constantinople in 1919
before Ataturk shut down the courts
set up by the Turks themselves
to judge the criminals in their midst.
That would be the first step towards justice,
the first move towards a punishment to fit the crime,
not the end but the start of a process—
provided vengeance wasn't its motive.
But you can't do that,
the perpetrators of the abomination are all dead.
As for restitution, indemnity, territory,
they are of secondary importance today,
for the time being quite out of reach.
You Armenians have moved on.
Justice can be accomplished now
only if the present-day government of Turkey admits
that their predecessors really did this execrable thing.
Then those events will take their place in the past.
You and your Armenian people
will be free from your anger, your grief,
and the weight of injustice that burdens your hearts;
and the Turks will be loosed from the shame that gnaws at their souls
and blocks them from knowing who they are,
from knowing who you are,
from knowing *me*.
Horizons will open before you both;
the community of nations will welcome you.

But the Turks don't see it that way.

Only grace will enable them to see it.
Neither vengeance on your part
nor denial on theirs
will solve anything.
Forgiveness is the only way forward.
It alone can remove the resentment and pride
that keeps your two peoples bound together
like Siamese twins in mortal combat;
it alone can alter the configuration
of forces on earth and in heaven.
It must come from the heart,
in obedience to me, by my power,
by the power of my Cross.
You must offer grace.
Grace was never taught by Mohammed—
the Turks don't understand such a thing.
(And who can truly understand grace?)
As for you, you have received my grace,
and you know it—
so you can offer it.
Then I can act;
then in time they will stop trying to destroy you.

I will try to believe;
I will try to obey.

*Trust me, says the Lord*

## XI

Out in the Syrian desert east of Aleppo
The wind kicks up dust-swirls,
Loose sand blows fitfully.
Sun glares on the rocks,
The bone-dry ground bakes.
Everything is yellow, scorched.
A lizard skitters.
Silence.

A scrubby bush over there—
Isn't it moving?
I think I hear voices.
Are those voices?
No, it's only the wind.
I thought I heard voices.
It's the wind, I tell you.
There's no one for miles,
Just sand and rocks, a few caves.
This is the Syrian desert, remember?
No one lives here.

*No one ever lived here*

## XII

Come, Lord—
*Maranatha*

# PART IV

## THE PEACH-MOON

I awoke at four. An enormous peach
had fallen from the tree of night
and landed on the hill across the valley.
Still drugged with sleep, I stretched to reach
the ripe fruit, then drew back in fright:
no peach, this:
*out there, eyeing the valley,*
*Earth's foster-child squatted, huge globe*
*of rock, a mass of matter: Moon.*
*No green here, no life. This rock hunk*
*had circled earth for eons, orb*
*dappled with craters, a pocked stone*
*ball hung in emptiness, chunk*
*of the primordial planet flung*
*outward, spun into a sphere*
*by powers our keen race names*
*but cannot match—Moon you are, sung*
*by bards, revered by lovers, who hear*
*in your repetitive refrain*
*the changeless mystery of being,*
*pedal point of the varying verses*
*of earth's hymn to her Creator,*
*the cyclic twinned with linear becoming,*
*music of the One who cherishes*
*His much-loved handiwork forever,*
*yet leaves his creatures free to change,*
*to become other, to fall, rise,*
*and, regarding our poor race, to die,*
*then grace receive (or not), so to range*
*Heaven, meet God's clear gaze,*
*like phoenixes from ash to fly*

*up, soar on Wind, cruise*
*in company of swift angels*
*the open spaces of creation.*

I shuddered. Had I dreamed? What news
was this? What jubilant tales
was Moon singing? What intuition
of reality was this ripe peach,
fallen from night's tree, sending me,
as it sank into dark behind the hill?

So I mused briefly. Then sleep's clutch
gripped me, night claimed the valley,
the vision melted into Lethe's deep well.

## WORDS

Words cannot capture the motion of shadows
On the grass, or the rustle of leaves in the wind;
The flutter of butterflies eludes their grasp,
Nor have they purchase on the vagrant clouds.
What they can do is make symbolic worlds,
Like a mirror reflecting objects in a room;
The worlds are like an echo, not unreal,
But made of sounds and signs instead of objects.
By naming objects, words make particulars
Familiar; namer and named become present
To each other, beings are known. So language,
Though immaterial, bodies forth meaning;
The word gives objects immaterial form.
My cat, named Clovis, processes by instinct
What his senses tell him; I do the same
By cognition, enabled by speech.
For God the Creator, word and form are one,
As He is in himself; what he speaks, is.
Made in his image, we speak not the world
But its image. Yet, by our inventions,
We bring it forth symbolically, like the mirror,
And lift from anonymity the primal forms,
Making them ours. The clouds and butterflies
And rustling leaves are here for me by words;
Language, as complement to Being, translates
Beings to my mind, binds us, so making them
Available to love.
O shadows, butterflies,
Clouds, leaves, you are created by Another,
Whose Presence—Being—appears through you.
My words, unlike His, cannot create you,

Nor can I possess you; but I can name
And know you, behold your beauty, love you;
And loving you, I can love the One
Who made you, and give him glory.

## RAINDROPS

All night long rain muttered on the rooftops.
The drops were voices from childhood.
There were later voices too.
The voices are faint,
I am old now,
Even the voices from years not long gone are growing faint.

It's how it is when you say goodbye to your beloved on a runway.
The plane lifts off and climbs,
Then bends back to find its direction westward,
So that for a moment you think you see her face in a window,
You think you see her waving;
Then the plane keeps climbing into emptiness
And grows smaller and smaller till it is no bigger than a gnat,
And your heart grows smaller and smaller till it is no bigger than a gnat.

*You are alone on the tarmac*

Yes, the light of God's Kingdom heats your spirit,
It lifts your eyes beyond the gnat disappearing
Into the enormous sun setting on this life;
Yes, your years will be redeemed, you know that.
But your heart as you stand now holding your breath on the tarmac,
As you strain to hear the voices muttering in the raindrops on the roof-tiles
('ping', 'plop', 'smack'),
Is empty.

The voices in the raindrops are fading.
You strain to hear your beloved's voice among them,
To hear her as she used to speak in the fullness of your lives.
Oh, it was like *spring water!*

Now the rain has stopped.

## GHOSTS

Tonight the moon is a fried egg *sunny side over.*
The flannel sky muffles sound.
A few ghosts are sitting in moon-white lawn chairs
Around the table in the garden.
The moonlight is like whey;
The ghosts sip it thoughtfully.

Then a neighbor's dog starts hammering a nail on the night.
The startled ghosts stop their ears.
*Yapyapyap!*
Then abruptly the yapping stops.

Silence.

The ghosts are still uneasy.
Their breath troubles the acacia nearby.
Staring at their dim reflections
On the glass-topped table,
They think how things once were.
They remember when the moon was a fried egg
*Sunny side up.*
"Memories become bones and blood,"
They think to themselves,
Shivering.

But ghosts don't have bones and blood.

## SHAPES IN THE MIST

I'm after something. I'm reaching out
To the mist on the horizon. I see shapes
In the mist, men like trees walking.
I know they've got bodies,
They're not ghosts,
I know they're going somewhere,
But I just can't make them out,
I just can't get hold of them.

I ask an odd question:
What can I give them to eat?
Suppose I give them my sorrows—
Would they take on solidity then?
Or my achievements, poor as they are?
But surely they've got their own sorrows,
Their own achievements—
Mine would just weigh them down.
How about my mundane tasks:
Letters, bills, planning, shopping, feeding our cats?
But surely they've got their own tasks to worry about
As they grope their way in the mist—
Why should I burden them with more?
And my joys?
Perhaps here I'm onto something.
Perhaps they're having trouble breathing
And my joys would help them.

What do the shapes see as they look in my direction?
Perhaps I'm in the mist too,
Like a tree walking.
Perhaps they wonder if I'm substantial.
Am I substantial?
Well, if I could reach them, I'd *prove* to them I am—yes sir!
But I can't seem to reach them, that's the problem.
But maybe just *wanting* to reach them proves I'm substantial—
Just my *longing!*
Why, maybe my longing proves *they're* substantial too,
Though they don't seem to be more than insubstantial shapes in the mist!
Actually, when you think about it,
What really are those shapes out there?
I mean—*really?*

## BEYOND THE STARS

I reside between the rough bark
And the burning stars.
I embrace trees and say, "I love you."
The remote stars I consider with awe,
But it's hard to say to them, "I love you."
Yet they're lodged in me,
Their light fills my eyes.
I can't touch them like the rough bark,
Yet they burn in my belly.
What they are in themselves,
Materially,
I consider thoughtfully and marvel,
Because I come from there;
But it's their beauty burns inside me,
Not just their atoms:
It radiates glory,
It's the invisible made visible,
Like the waving trees that make visible the wind.
That beauty is Home,
I belong there;
With my heart I know it,
As I know the rough bark with my hand.
To this that is beyond the stars,
To that of which this beauty is a sign,
A Word,
I can say—and I want to say—
"I love you."

# PART V

## THE ZINC SKY

In the zinc sky,
Sun glows.
Dry leaves fill potholes in the road.
The chestnut leaves are rusting.
Plum trees are dropping their fruit,
The blackberries on the thorn-bushes are nearly ripe.

You remember how it was when you were a boy.
When you were a boy, you didn't know how it was.
What you did then, you simply *did*;
Understanding eluded you.
The plate of your heart was being engraved with a fine point,
But you knew nothing of all that.
*Then*, you *did*;
*Now*, you *remember* what you did.
But do you understand?
Recollection is recognition;
It is the second dimension in the making of a life.
The third dimension is meaning.
Surely there can be no meaning without hope.
If, remembering, you are bitter,
Or hollowed out by regrets and self-hatred,
Or caught in the quicksand of resentment,
Or trapped at the bottom of an empty well
Where your voice is only an echo;
And if, ahead, you see no open door
Through which light might come,
Or singing,
Or persons from the past to welcome you,
You are of all persons most to be pitied.
The past is a dream from which you are waking up;
The future is a nightmare from which you won't awake.

Your life was not meant to be a flat balloon;
The third dimension is still out there for you,
If you want it.
But you won't find in yourself air to pump up your lungs.
Breath is God's gift.
If you don't raise your head to heaven and cry "Help!",
You will die.

In the zinc sky,
Sun glows.
Yes, the clouds are gathering in the west,
Night is coming.
But the light of that great Star still shines,
Illuminating the world,
Illuminating you.

Why don't you open your eyes?

# CLOUD-DRAMA AT A STORMY EVENING'S CLOSE

*The heavens declare the glory of God;*
*The skies proclaim the work of his hands.*
*Day after day they pour forth speech;*
*Night after night they display knowledge.*
*There is no speech or language*
*Where their voice is not heard.*
*Their voice goes out into all the earth,*
*Their words to the end of the world.*
(Psalm 19:1–4)


Vaporous ice-banks bulge on the orange horizon,
More bulge beyond
Westward
Out, out—
Glaciers, floes, packs, crevasses,
Hydrangeas in abyssal space
Flowering.
In front of the ice-banks, layers,
Layers and levels,
Piles, pyramids, packs,
Boulders,
Debris-heaps and moraine sliding eastward,
Tumbling
In, in,
Surging from the taffeta rim of the earth,
Filling the blue:
Ranks,
Orders,
Rows,
Mountains, masses,
Cliffs towering up to dreadful heights

(And here, there, birds soaring,
Floating like letters, crying,
*"We live! We live!"*)—
And all these vanilla legions going lemon and liquorice,
All these cohorts of cloud,
All these battalions are heaved out of west by the dying sun,
Borne by the planet's currents,
Carved by the wind's keen fingers:
Forms tracing air,
Configuring sky,
Developing depth
On the flat sheet of heaven,
On the blank blue canvas—
Thus is void named,
Infinity shaped,
As words actualize thought
And make mind known.

This whole world of vapor *breathes*,
This woolly duplicate of earth's rock *flows*.
And within this enormous metamorphic realization,
Within these resolving and dissolving masses,
These floats, shapes, shards and mighty puffs,
Copies of circuses of living creatures
Also glide down wind's broad streams,
Wordlessly ravelling and unravelling,
Beasts in silent revel:

Elephants, manatees, snails, barracuda,
Turtles, crocodiles, porpoises, boars,
Gorillas, dogs, giraffes, lions,
Swordfish, buffalo, goats, hares—
Going, going,
On, on,
Going,
Cotton forms unfolding down wind's way,
Down boundless air,
Down air,

Mimes on sky's stage,
Voluminous cloud-beasts,
Soundless,
Substantial,
Insubstantial,
Weightless,
Wafting on infinity's face.

*In stillness they pass,*
*Wondrous;*
*They glide*
*Without seeming to move;*
*They drift,*
*Float,*
*Pass,*
*Pass by,*
*Pass away,*
*Conjuring invisible worlds.*

The color!
Back at the verge of the planet,
Where fires are stoked to consume blue day,
The face of the monumental ice-bank
Is flat, opaque, dark, a lead plate
Bolted to the furnace of the western sky.
Fire-streaks running on the furnace edge
Outline the cloud-stones piled above.
From the sun's veiled hub fan light-spokes
Striking into earth's loamy rim
And up through heaven's cavern.
Fields of poppies flare in the dome,
Orange in the heights, red by the vault's base.
The sun, crushed by ice-floes,
Bleeds out its life across the sky.
High near the zenith, above the haemorrhage,
The cirrus are cream-swirls on a platter;
Below sits a peach-tinted dish with fruit;
Lower still, under tilting sun-rays,

Lie lumps of cumulous now extinguished:
Mussels clumped on tide-washed rocks.

The clouds cruise by like ocean combers,
Foaming, dissipating, vanishing;
They pass through colors as through stages of life,
Then flatten into darkness.
On several planes they advance,
At different speeds,
In varying configurations:
Freight-trains on unseen levees,
Persimmon-coloured;
Convoys in the middle tracts of sky,
Salmon-tinted;
Barges on the low, slow currents,
Charcoal-toned.
As on a stage, where movable panels glide back and forth,
The huge shapes cross and pass, unhurried,
Each level on its course,
A saga unfolding:
*Earth's dream.*

And there, far off, lie inland seas and bays,
Lakes, lagoons, fiords,
Great rents in the darkening cloud-cape,
Blue holes opening onto heaven,
Where feathers and sheep's wool float serenely,
While nearer, by the bay-shores,
Tangerine tufts wind-surf on the void.

Westward, behind the leaden citadel,
Ladders of light prop up the sinking sun,
Whose molten disc, a circular saw,
Cuts through the cloud-mass and arcs out beneath.
Below burns the rose furnace;
Beyond, way out, in layered bands
Stacked against encroaching night,
Lie streaks of gold and cinnabar,
Blue powder melting into green.

In languages of cloud, sky speaks
To listening hills and plains,
To deserts, oceans, mountain ranges
Of the tangible earth, imprinting codes
And patterns on their masses,
Revelations of reality.
For all things coming to be
Are launched into time,
Grow, peak,
Shrink, die,
Go,
Are gone,
Like clouds.
Yet under their courses,
Behind their trajectories
And transformations,
Stands the Poet who utters them,
Whose speech sounds in the cloud-reams
Rolling through air.

He imagines in a thousand idioms,
Declining the endings of cloud-speech,
Creating correspondences and rhymes,
Declaiming magisterially
Grand cadences of matter—
So the Poet discloses by this mummers' play
The Primordial Word.

Down here on solid earth,
Like a farmer tilling land,
The poet works the field of his empty page,
Following the Master.
He scatters words in rows,
Like seeds in furrows,
For the nourishment
Of the rare, bold hearts,
Untamed and wild,
That dare to love.

As cloud-words articulate fathomless sky,
So the poet's scribblings,
Tracing his sheet,
Limn forms on its blank white void,
Draw shapes from its bottomless well,
Intimating meaning.

Signs, these—
Signs like the choruses of vapor
Appearing out of somewhere,
(Nothing appears out of nowhere),
Singing silent hymns of praise
To the glory of God,
Seminal Creator,
Who sustains in the radiance
Of the love we name "beauty",
The brief incandescence
Of creatures.

www.ingramcontent.com/pod-product-compliance
Lightning Source LLC
LaVergne TN
LVHW051704080426
835511LV00017B/2731